What Smells?

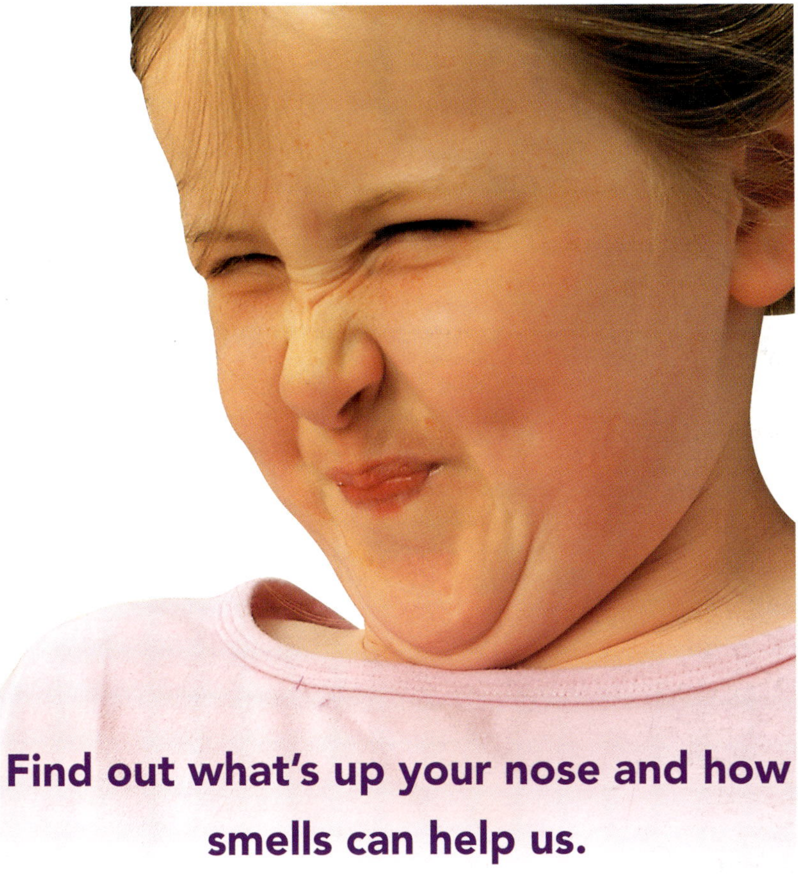

Find out what's up your nose and how smells can help us.

by Susan Piper

 800-445-5985
www.etacuisenaire.com

What Smells?
ISBN 0-7406-4139-5
ETA 382201

ETA/Cuisenaire • Vernon Hills, IL 60061-1862
800-445-5985 • www.etacuisenaire.com

Series © 2006 by ETA/Cuisenaire®

Original version published by Nelson Australia Pty Limited (2002). This edition is published by arrangement with Thomson Learning Australia.

All rights reserved. No part of this publication may be reproduced, stored in a retrieval system, or transmitted, in any form or by any means, electronic, mechanical, photocopying, recording, or otherwise, without the prior written permission of the publisher.

ETA/Cuisenaire
Manager of Product Development: Mary Watanabe
Creative Services Manager: Barry Daniel Petersen
Production Manager: Jeanette Pletsch
Lead Editor: Betty Hey
Copy Editor: Barbara Wrobel
Production Artist: Diana Chiropolos
Graphic Designer: Amy Endlich

Photographs on pp. i, iii, iv, 1–2, 7–9, 11–21 24–28, and cover by Fotograffiti
Illustrations on pp. 3, 5–8, 10–11, 21, and 23 by Guy Holt Design

Teacher consultant: Garry Chapman, Ivanhoe Grammar School

Printed in China.

06 07 08 09 10 11 12 13 14 15   10 9 8 7 6 5 4 3 2 1

Contents

Chapter One
What's Up Your Nose?   1

Chapter Two
Smelling Stuff   7

Chapter Three
Smells You Can Taste   13

Chapter Four
Your Nose Knows Best   17

Chapter Five
Bugs Can Make You Smell!   21

Chapter Six
Good Smells   25

Glossary 28
Index 28

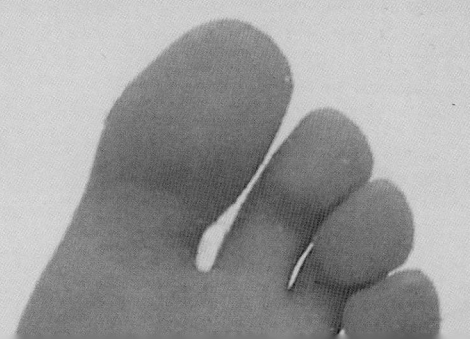

Chapter One

What's Up Your Nose?

Do you know what smells are or why you can smell them? These are big questions. To find the answers, let's start with your nose. Sniff, sniff.

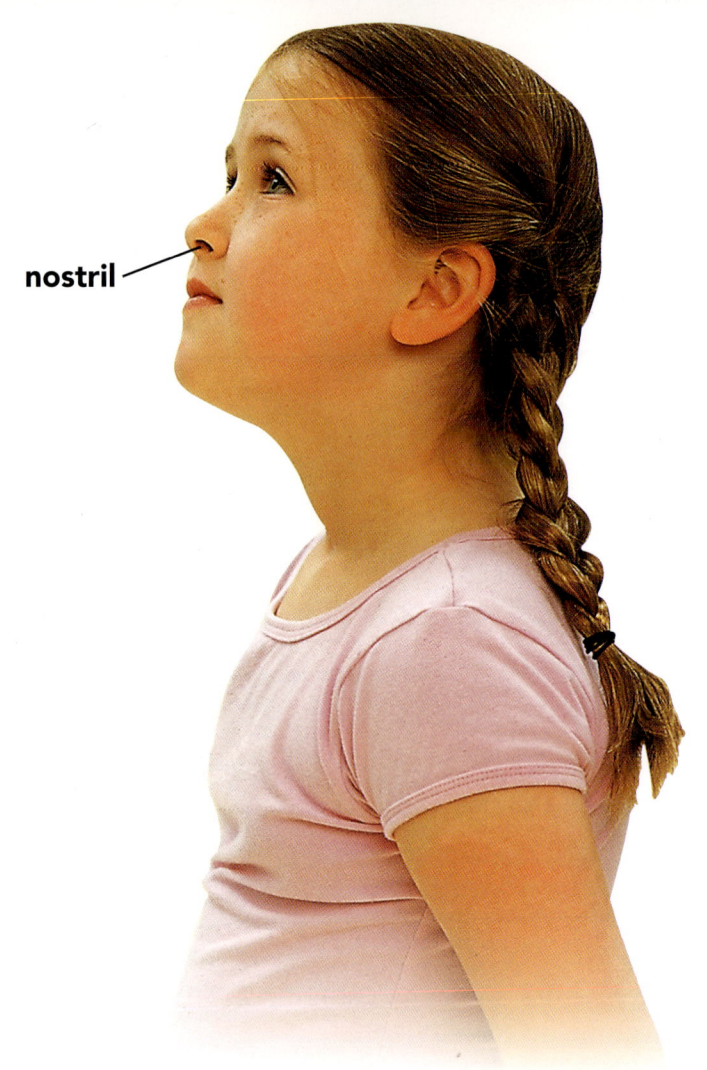

nostril

Smells are in the air around you. When you breathe in, air and smells enter your nose through two holes. These holes are called nostrils.

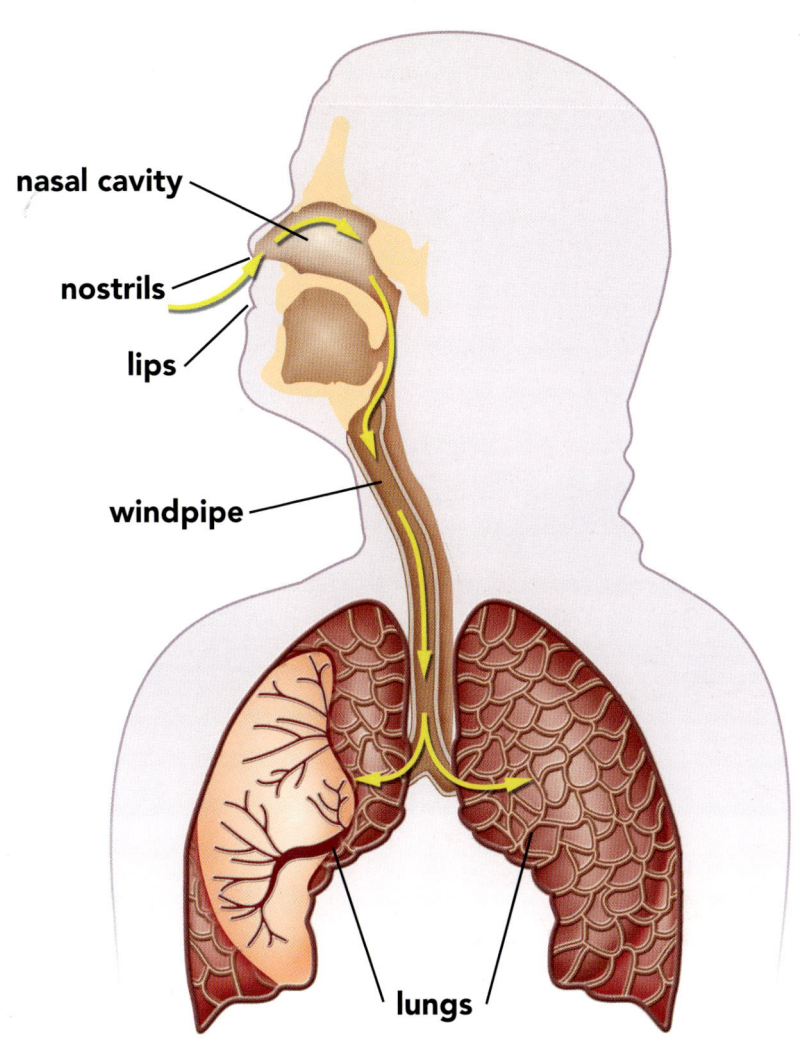

The air goes through your nostrils to your nasal [NAY-zal] **cavity**. Then it goes down your windpipe to your lungs.

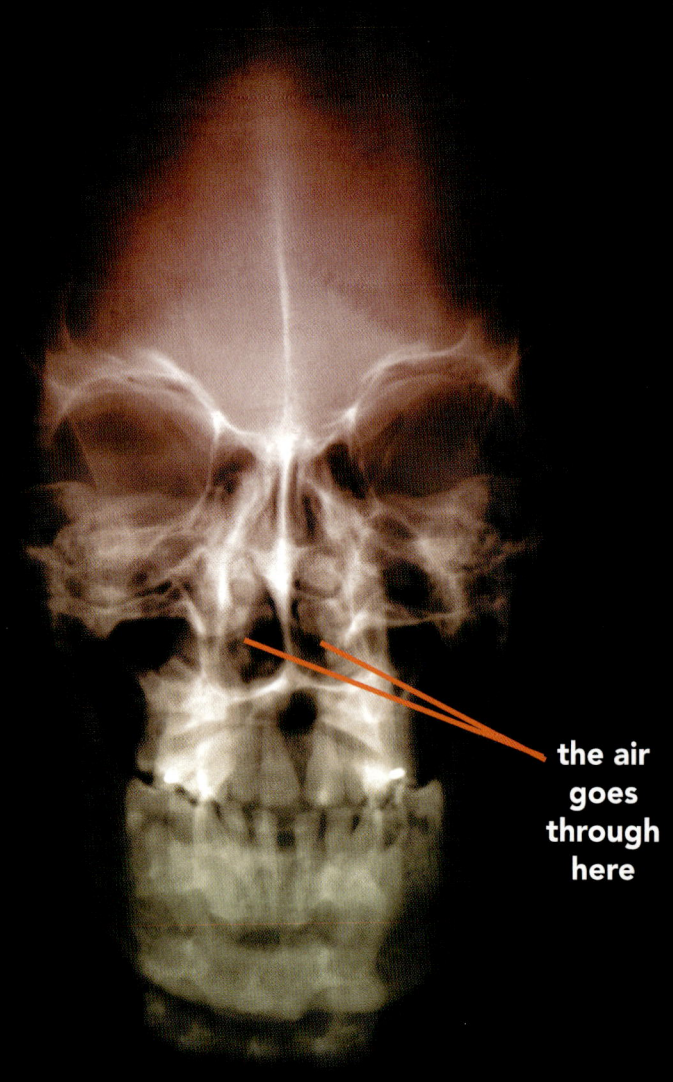

the air goes through here

This is an **x-ray** of a human skull. You can see the place where the air goes in through the nostrils. But the x-ray doesn't show what's inside the nostrils.

On the inside of your nostrils, there is a sticky layer. It's called the **mucous** [MEW-kus] **membrane**. There are also tiny hairs—thousands of them!

Dust and germs get stuck in the mucous membrane and the hairs. That's how your nose helps to clean the air that you breathe.

Chapter Two

Smelling Stuff

Dust and germs aren't the only things in the air. There are smells in the air, too.

Smells are tiny **chemicals** [KEM-i-kals]. You can't see them, but they float in the air around you.

When you breathe air into your nose,
smells are breathed in with it.

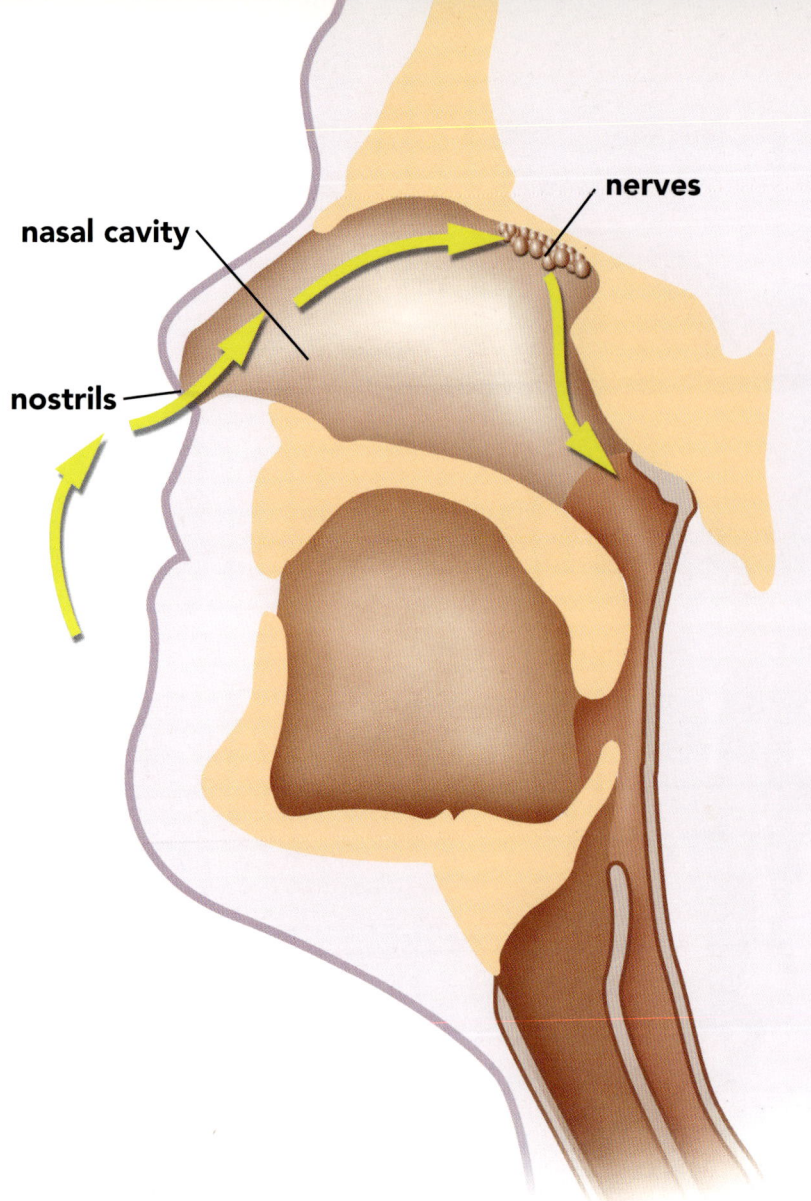

The smells float up to the back of your nose. There are special **nerves** in this spot. The nerves decide what the smells are.

The nerves send a message to your brain, telling your brain if the smell is beautiful —or horrible. They can even tell your brain if the smell comes from something that will taste good.

People can't always agree on what smells good and what smells bad. Just as we all like different clothes and colors, we all like different smells and tastes.

Chapter Three

Smells You Can Taste

When we smell something we've eaten before, our brain remembers whether we liked the taste or not.

But if you have a cold and your nose is blocked, you can't smell very well. When you can't smell very well, you can't taste very well, either.

Let's do a taste test. You'll need a piece of potato and a piece of apple. A friend will have to help, because you can't look at what you're eating!

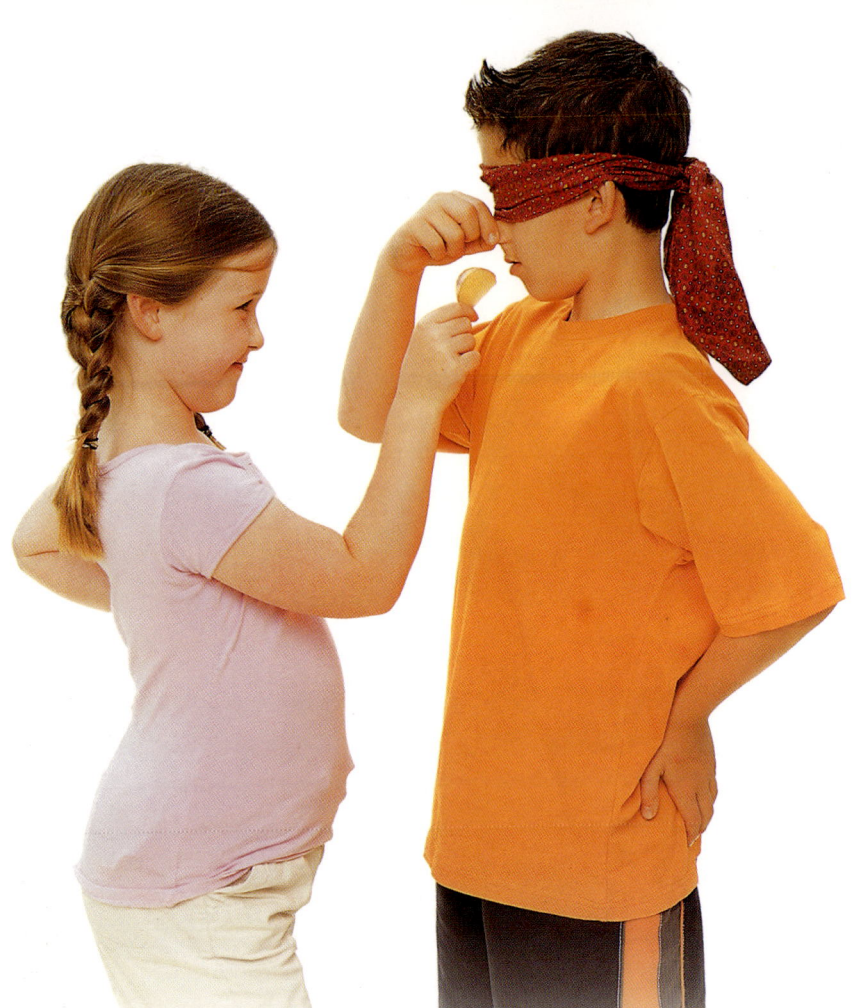

- Put on a blindfold and pinch your nose.
- Get your friend to give you the pieces of food to eat, one at a time.

Can you tell the difference between the flavors easily? No, because smell is a big part of taste.

Chapter Four

Your Nose Knows Best

Flavor isn't the only thing your nose can help with. What are some other ways your nose can use smell to help you?

It can stop you from eating food that has gone bad. Sour milk looks just the same as fresh milk. But if you smell the milk, you'll know if it has gone bad.

Your nose can also warn you if there is a fire. And it will let you know if you have stepped in something smelly!

Your nose will even tell you when it's time to take a bath. Or when it's time to give your smelly old running shoes a wash.

Chapter Five

Bugs Can Make You Smell!

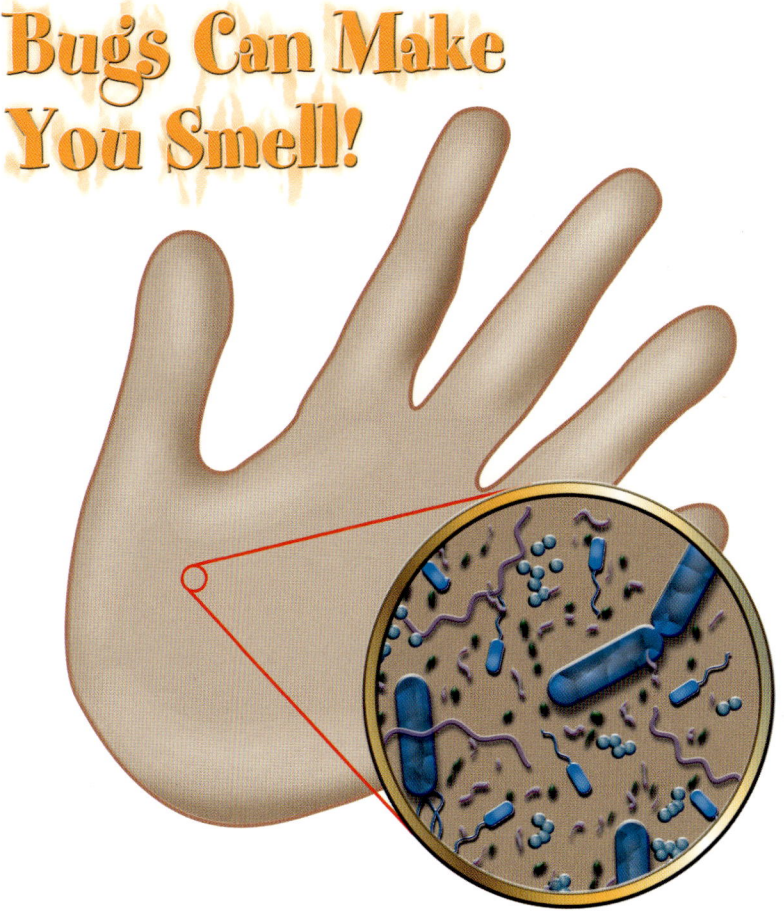

Tiny bugs grow on your skin. It sounds horrible, but it's true! Did you know that these bugs can give you smelly skin?

Your feet do a lot of work. They are inside shoes much of the time, and they can get hot and sweaty.

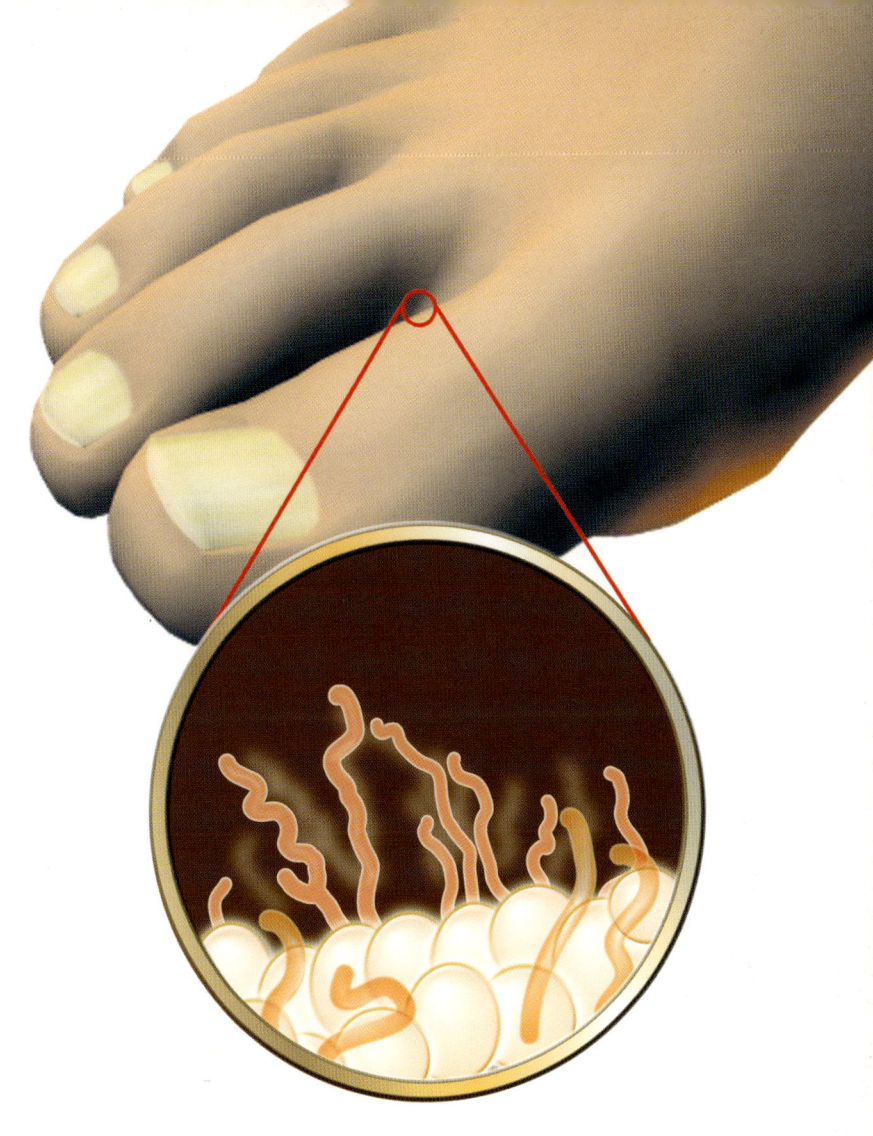

The bugs like their home to be hot and sweaty. They grow and **multiply**. Then they get more and more smelly. And that makes your feet stink!

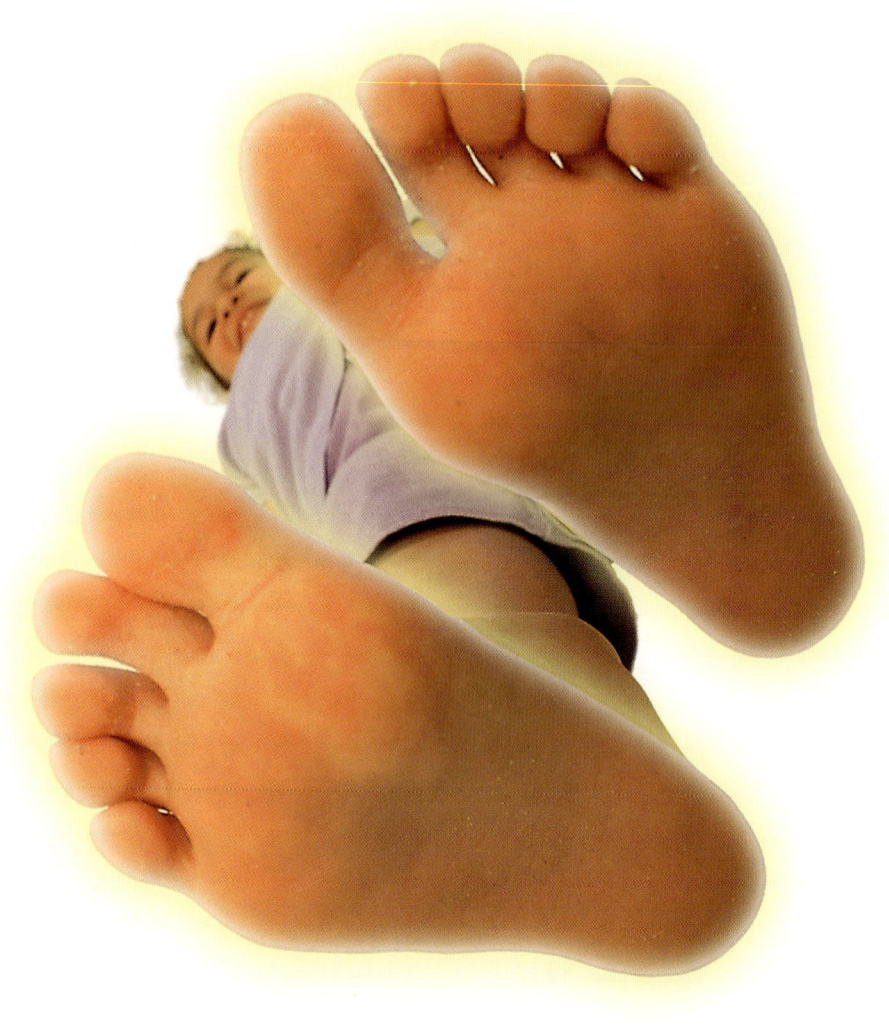

It's a good idea to start every day with clean feet. That way the bad smells don't have time to build up!

Chapter Six

Good Smells

Some smells can change how you feel. Did you know that the smell of peppermint can help to make you feel better if you are carsick?

There are smells that make people happy.
Other smells remind you of things.
Sniffing seashells can make you think of
the seashore.

So lift your nose and sniff the air. What smells are there?

Glossary

cavity a hollow place
chemicals [KEM-i-kals] what substances are made of
mucous [MEW-kus] **membrane** a moist lining inside some parts of the body
multiply to grow in number
nerves fibers that send messages between the brain and other parts of the body
x-ray a special kind of photograph of the inside of the body

Index

breathe 2, 6, 9
bugs 21, 23
chemicals 8
flavor 16, 17
mucous membrane 5, 6
nerves 10, 11
nose 1, 2, 6, 9, 10, 14, 16, 17, 19, 20, 27
nostrils 2, 3, 4, 5, 10
taste 11, 12, 13, 14, 15, 16
x-ray 4

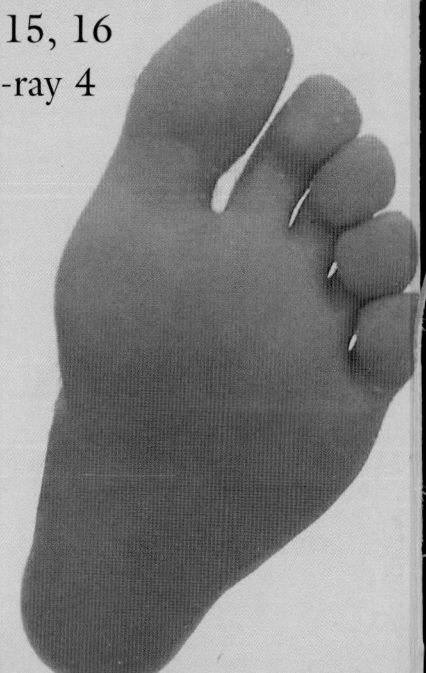